Funfetti Cake Cookbook 101

A Vibrant Collection of Creative and Delicious Funfetti Cake Recipes for Every Occasion

While every precaution has been taken in the preparation of this book, the publisher assumes no responsibility for errors or omissions, or for damages resulting from the use of the information contained herein.

FUNFETTI CAKE COOKBOOK 101

First edition. January 20, 2024.

Copyright © 2024 john ahmad.

ISBN: 979-8223037125

Written by john ahmad.

John Ahmad

Chapter 1: Introduction to Funfetti Cakes

What is a Funfetti cake?

Funfetti cakes are delightful, whimsical creations that bring joy and color to any occasion. At their core, Funfetti cakes are traditional vanilla cakes infused with a vibrant explosion of rainbow sprinkles. As the cake bakes, the sprinkles distribute throughout the batter, resulting in a confetti-like appearance once sliced. Funfetti cakes are beloved for their festive aesthetics and delightful flavor, making them a favorite choice for birthdays, celebrations, and any day that calls for a touch of fun.

The history and popularity of Funfetti cakes

The origins of Funfetti cakes can be traced back to the mid-20th century when sprinkles gained widespread popularity in baking. The Pillsbury Company, known for their ready-to-bake products, introduced Funfetti cake mix to the market in 1989. Since then, Funfetti cakes have become a cherished part of American baking culture, adored by both children and adults alike.

The appeal of Funfetti cakes lies not only in their visual appeal but also in the nostalgic and celebratory atmosphere they evoke. From birthday parties to graduation celebrations, Funfetti cakes have a way of bringing people together and creating lasting memories. The playful nature of these cakes has inspired countless variations, adaptations, and creative uses of Funfetti in the world of baking.

Essential tools and ingredients for Funfetti baking

To embark on your Funfetti baking journey, there are a few essential tools and ingredients that will help you achieve the best results. Here's a list of what you'll need:

- Mixing bowls: Have a variety of sizes on hand to accommodate different recipes and mixing needs.

- Electric mixer or stand mixer: While you can mix Funfetti cake batter by hand, an electric mixer will make the process smoother and more efficient.

- Cake pans: Opt for round cake pans in various sizes to create layered cakes. Non-stick pans or those lined with parchment paper are recommended for easy release.

- Whisk or spatula: These utensils are essential for combining ingredients and ensuring a smooth batter.

- Cooling racks: Allow your Funfetti cakes to cool evenly by placing them on cooling racks after removing them from the oven.

- Funfetti sprinkles: The star ingredient that gives Funfetti cakes their signature appearance. Choose high-quality rainbow sprinkles to achieve vibrant colors and a delightful crunch.

- Vanilla extract: A key flavoring agent in Funfetti cakes. Opt for pure vanilla extract for the best flavor.

- All-purpose flour: The base ingredient for Funfetti cake batter. Make sure it is fresh and properly measured.

- Baking powder and baking soda: Leavening agents that ensure your Funfetti cakes rise properly.

- Salt: Enhances the overall flavor of the cake and balances the sweetness.

- Unsalted butter: Provides richness and moisture to the cake batter. Make sure it is at room temperature for easy incorporation.

- Granulated sugar: Sweetens the cake and helps create a tender texture.

- Eggs: Bind the ingredients together and contribute to the structure of the cake.

- Whole milk or buttermilk: Adds moisture and richness to the cake batter.

- Frosting and additional decorations: While not essential,

frosting and extra sprinkles can take your Funfetti cakes to the next level. Consider buttercream, cream cheese frosting, or even a glaze for your creations.

Now that you're equipped with an understanding of Funfetti cakes, their history, and the necessary tools and ingredients, it's time to dive into the wonderful world of Funfetti baking. In the following chapters, we'll explore a variety of Funfetti cake recipes, variations, and creative ideas that will make your taste buds dance with delight. Get ready to unleash your inner baker and bring the magic of Funfetti into your kitchen!

Chapter 2: Classic Funfetti Cakes

In this chapter, we'll explore the timeless charm of classic Funfetti cakes. From the traditional recipe to exciting variations and tips for achieving impeccable sprinkle distribution, get ready to indulge in the joyous world of Funfetti baking.

Traditional Funfetti cake recipe

Ingredients:

- 2 ½ cups all-purpose flour
- 2 ½ teaspoons baking powder
- ½ teaspoon salt
- 1 cup unsalted butter, at room temperature
- 2 cups granulated sugar
- 4 large eggs
- 2 teaspoons vanilla extract
- 1 cup whole milk
- ½ cup rainbow sprinkles

Instructions:

1. Preheat your oven to 350°F (175°C) and prepare two 9-inch round cake pans by greasing them and lining the bottoms with parchment paper.
2. In a medium-sized bowl, whisk together the flour, baking powder, and salt. Set aside.
3. In a separate large mixing bowl, cream the butter and granulated sugar together using an electric mixer until light and

fluffy. This should take about 3-4 minutes.

4. Add the eggs one at a time, beating well after each addition. Stir in the vanilla extract.

5. Gradually add the dry ingredients to the butter mixture, alternating with the milk. Begin and end with the dry ingredients, mixing just until combined after each addition.

6. Gently fold in the rainbow sprinkles, being careful not to overmix and cause them to bleed too much into the batter.

7. Divide the batter evenly between the prepared cake pans, smoothing the tops with a spatula.

8. Bake in the preheated oven for 25-30 minutes or until a toothpick inserted into the center of the cakes comes out clean.

9. Remove the cakes from the oven and let them cool in the pans for 10 minutes. Then, transfer them to a wire rack to cool completely before frosting.

Variations on classic Funfetti flavors

While the traditional Funfetti cake recipe is delightful on its own, you can also experiment with different flavor variations to add an extra twist to your creations. Here are a few ideas to get you started:

Chocolate Funfetti Cake: Replace ½ cup of the all-purpose flour with cocoa powder to infuse a rich chocolate flavor into the cake. You can also consider using chocolate sprinkles in addition to the rainbow sprinkles for a dual-colored effect.

Lemon Funfetti Cake: Add 2 tablespoons of freshly grated lemon zest to the cake batter for a refreshing citrusy twist. Pair it with a lemon-flavored frosting for a burst of tangy goodness.

Almond Funfetti Cake: Substitute 1 teaspoon of the vanilla extract with almond extract to infuse the cake with a delicate nutty flavor. Top it off with an almond-flavored buttercream for a harmonious combination.

Strawberry Funfetti Cake: Fold in 1 cup of finely diced fresh strawberries into the batter for a fruity surprise. Consider using strawberry-flavored sprinkles for an added burst of strawberry goodness.

Feel free to unleash your creativity and experiment with other flavor combinations that excite your taste buds. The possibilities are endless!

Tips for achieving the perfect sprinkle distribution

Achieving an even distribution of sprinkles throughout your Funfetti cake can be a challenge. Here are some tips to help you achieve that picture-perfect sprinkle effect:

Use jimmies or nonpareils: Jimmies (long, rod-shaped sprinkles) or nonpareils (tiny round sprinkles) work best for Funfetti cakes. These types of sprinkles hold their shape and color during baking, resulting in a more defined sprinkle appearance.

Toss the sprinkles in flour: Before folding the sprinkles into the batter, lightly coat them with a small amount of flour. This helps prevent them from sinking to the bottom of the cake during baking.

Gently fold in the sprinkles: When incorporating the sprinkles into the batter, use a gentle folding motion. Overmixing can cause the colors to bleed and result in a less distinct sprinkle pattern.

Distribute sprinkles evenly: When dividing the batter between the cake pans, sprinkle a small handful of additional sprinkles onto each layer. This ensures that the sprinkles are distributed evenly throughout the cakes.

Add sprinkles to the frosting: To enhance the Funfetti experience, consider adding sprinkles to the frosting as well. Lightly press them onto the sides and top of the frosted cake for a festive and fun appearance.

With these tips in mind, you're well on your way to creating classic Funfetti cakes that are not only delicious but also visually stunning. Enjoy the process and the delightful surprise of rainbow sprinkles in every bite.

Chapter 3: Funfetti Cupcakes and Mini Treats

In this chapter, we'll explore the world of Funfetti cupcakes and mini treats. These bite-sized delights are perfect for parties, gatherings, or simply enjoying a single serving of Funfetti goodness. Get ready to indulge in irresistible Funfetti cupcakes, adorable bite-sized cake pops, and delectable Funfetti donuts and muffins.

Irresistible Funfetti Cupcakes

Ingredients for Funfetti Cupcakes:

- 1 ¼ cups all-purpose flour
- 1 ½ teaspoons baking powder
- ¼ teaspoon salt
- ½ cup unsalted butter, at room temperature
- 1 cup granulated sugar
- 2 large eggs
- 1 teaspoon vanilla extract
- ½ cup whole milk
- ⅓ cup rainbow sprinkles

Instructions:

1. Preheat your oven to 350°F (175°C) and line a cupcake tin with paper liners.
2. In a medium-sized bowl, whisk together the flour, baking powder, and salt. Set aside.
3. In a separate large mixing bowl, cream the butter and granulated sugar together using an electric mixer until light and

fluffy. This should take about 2-3 minutes.

4. Add the eggs one at a time, beating well after each addition. Stir in the vanilla extract.

5. Gradually add the dry ingredients to the butter mixture, alternating with the milk. Begin and end with the dry ingredients, mixing just until combined after each addition.

6. Gently fold in the rainbow sprinkles, being careful not to overmix and cause them to bleed too much into the batter.

7. Spoon the batter into the prepared cupcake liners, filling each one about two-thirds full.

8. Bake in the preheated oven for 18-20 minutes or until a toothpick inserted into the center of a cupcake comes out clean.

9. Remove the cupcakes from the oven and let them cool in the tin for a few minutes. Then, transfer them to a wire rack to cool completely before frosting.

Once cooled, frost the cupcakes with your favorite frosting, such as vanilla buttercream or cream cheese frosting. For an extra touch, sprinkle some additional rainbow sprinkles on top of the frosting.

Bite-sized Funfetti Cake Pops

Ingredients for Funfetti Cake Pops:

- 1 batch of Funfetti cupcakes (from the previous recipe)
- 1 cup frosting (your choice of flavor)
- 12 ounces candy melts or white chocolate, for coating
- Rainbow sprinkles, for decoration
- Lollipop sticks or cake pop sticks

Instructions:

1. Crumble the cooled Funfetti cupcakes into fine crumbs using your hands or a fork.
2. In a large bowl, mix the cupcake crumbs with the frosting until well combined. The mixture should hold together when pressed.
3. Shape the mixture into small cake balls, about 1 inch in diameter. Place them on a parchment-lined baking sheet.
4. Insert a lollipop stick or cake pop stick into each cake ball, about halfway through. Place the baking sheet in the refrigerator for about 30 minutes to firm up the cake balls.
5. In the meantime, melt the candy melts or white chocolate according to the package instructions.
6. Remove the cake balls from the refrigerator. Dip each cake ball into the melted candy melts, allowing any excess coating to drip off. Decorate with rainbow sprinkles immediately after dipping, as the coating sets quickly.
7. Stick the cake pops upright into a foam block or place them back on the parchment-lined baking sheet to allow the coating to set completely.
8. Once the coating has hardened, your Funfetti cake pops are ready to be enjoyed!

Funfetti Donuts and Muffins

Ingredients for Funfetti Donuts:

- 1 ¾ cups all-purpose flour
- ½ cup granulated sugar
- 2 teaspoons baking powder
- ½ teaspoon salt
- ¾ cup whole milk
- 2 large eggs
- 2 tablespoons unsalted butter, melted
- 1 teaspoon vanilla extract
- ⅓ cup rainbow sprinkles
- Optional: powdered sugar glaze or chocolate glaze for topping

Instructions:

1. Preheat your oven to 375°F (190°C) and grease a donut pan or muffin tin.
2. In a large bowl, whisk together the flour, sugar, baking powder, and salt.
3. In a separate bowl, whisk together the milk, eggs, melted butter, and vanilla extract.
4. Pour the wet ingredients into the dry ingredients and stir until just combined. Be careful not to overmix.
5. Gently fold in the rainbow sprinkles.
6. Spoon the batter into the greased donut pan or muffin tin, filling each cavity about three-quarters full.
7. Bake in the preheated oven for 12-15 minutes for donuts or 15-18 minutes for muffins, or until a toothpick inserted into the center comes out clean.
8. Remove from the oven and let the donuts or muffins cool in the pan for a few minutes before transferring them to a wire rack to

cool completely.

9. Once cooled, you can enjoy the Funfetti donuts and muffins as is or top them with a powdered sugar glaze or chocolate glaze for extra sweetness.

These Funfetti cupcakes, cake pops, donuts, and muffins are sure to delight both kids and adults alike. Their miniature sizes make them perfect for snacking or serving at parties, ensuring that every bite is a burst of colorful happiness. Let your imagination run wild with different frosting flavors, glazes, and decorative touches to make these mini treats even more visually appealing. Enjoy the delightful world of Funfetti in a smaller, bite-sized form!

Chapter 4: Decadent Funfetti Layer Cakes

In this chapter, we'll dive into the realm of decadent Funfetti layer cakes. These show-stopping creations are perfect for special occasions or whenever you want to impress your guests with a visually stunning and delicious dessert. We'll explore a variety of Funfetti layer cake recipes, different frosting options, and decorating techniques to achieve impressive results.

Show-stopping Funfetti Layer Cake Recipes

Funfetti Celebration Cake

Ingredients for Funfetti Cake Layers:

- 3 cups all-purpose flour
- 2 ½ teaspoons baking powder
- ½ teaspoon baking soda
- ½ teaspoon salt
- 1 ½ cups unsalted butter, at room temperature
- 2 ½ cups granulated sugar
- 5 large eggs
- 1 tablespoon vanilla extract
- 1 ½ cups buttermilk
- ½ cup rainbow sprinkles

Instructions:

1. Preheat your oven to 350°F (175°C). Grease and line three 8-inch round cake pans with parchment paper.

2. In a medium-sized bowl, whisk together the flour, baking powder, baking soda, and salt. Set aside.
3. In a separate large mixing bowl, cream the butter and granulated sugar together using an electric mixer until light and fluffy. This should take about 3-4 minutes.
4. Add the eggs one at a time, beating well after each addition. Stir in the vanilla extract.
5. Gradually add the dry ingredients to the butter mixture, alternating with the buttermilk. Begin and end with the dry ingredients, mixing just until combined after each addition.
6. Gently fold in the rainbow sprinkles, being careful not to overmix and cause them to bleed too much into the batter.
7. Divide the batter evenly among the prepared cake pans, smoothing the tops with a spatula.
8. Bake in the preheated oven for 25-30 minutes or until a toothpick inserted into the center of the cakes comes out clean.
9. Remove the cakes from the oven and let them cool in the pans for 10 minutes. Then, transfer them to a wire rack to cool completely before frosting.

Funfetti Layer Cake Frosting Options

Classic Vanilla Buttercream:

- 2 cups unsalted butter, at room temperature
- 4 cups powdered sugar
- 2 teaspoons vanilla extract
- Rainbow sprinkles, for decoration

In a large mixing bowl, beat the butter until creamy. Gradually add the powdered sugar, one cup at a time, and continue beating until light and fluffy. Stir in the vanilla extract. Frost the cooled Funfetti cake layers with the vanilla buttercream, stacking them on top of each other. Decorate the cake with rainbow sprinkles.

Cream Cheese Frosting:

- 16 ounces cream cheese, softened
- ½ cup unsalted butter, at room temperature
- 6 cups powdered sugar
- 2 teaspoons vanilla extract
- Rainbow sprinkles, for decoration

In a large mixing bowl, beat the cream cheese and butter until smooth and well combined. Gradually add the powdered sugar, one cup at a time, and continue beating until creamy. Stir in the vanilla extract. Frost the cooled Funfetti cake layers with the cream cheese frosting, stacking them on top of each other. Decorate the cake with rainbow sprinkles.

Decorating Techniques for Impressive Results

Naked Cake with Sprinkle Drip:

Frost the Funfetti layer cake with a thin layer of frosting between the layers. Use an offset spatula to create a rustic, "naked" look by scraping off excess frosting from the sides of the cake. Melt candy melts or white chocolate and drip it down the sides of the cake. Add a generous amount of rainbow sprinkles on top of the cake for an eye-catching finishing touch.

Ombré Funfetti Cake:

Prepare a larger batch of vanilla buttercream frosting. Divide it into three bowls and tint each portion with different shades of food coloring to create an ombré effect. Start with the darkest color at the bottom layer of the cake and gradually lighten the frosting as you go up. Use an offset spatula to blend the colors for a seamless transition. Finish with a sprinkle of rainbow sprinkles on top.

Funfetti Ruffle Cake:

Frost the Funfetti layer cake with a thin layer of frosting between the layers. Starting from the bottom, use a piping bag fitted with a petal tip to create ruffles around the sides of the cake. Work your way up, slightly overlapping the ruffles as you go. Finish with a dollop of frosting on top, adorned with rainbow sprinkles.

Remember, the sky's the limit when it comes to decorating your Funfetti layer cake. Feel free to experiment with different piping techniques, additional decorations like edible flowers or chocolate curls, or even themed designs based on the occasion. Let your creativity shine and create a masterpiece that not only tastes amazing but also leaves a lasting impression on your guests.

Chapter 5: Funfetti Cheesecakes and Pies

In this chapter, we'll explore the creamy and delightful world of Funfetti cheesecakes and pies. These rich and indulgent treats combine the beloved flavors of Funfetti with the smoothness of cream cheese or the comforting allure of pie. Discover how to create luscious Funfetti cheesecakes, explore variations of Funfetti pies, and learn tips for achieving the perfect texture in these delightful desserts.

Creamy and Delightful Funfetti Cheesecakes

Ingredients for Funfetti Cheesecake:

- 2 cups graham cracker crumbs
- ½ cup unsalted butter, melted
- 24 ounces cream cheese, softened
- 1 cup granulated sugar
- 3 large eggs
- 1 teaspoon vanilla extract
- 1 cup sour cream
- ½ cup rainbow sprinkles

Instructions:

Preheat your oven to 325°F (163°C). Grease a 9-inch springform pan.

1. In a medium-sized bowl, combine the graham cracker crumbs and melted butter until the crumbs are evenly coated.
2. Press the mixture into the bottom of the greased springform pan, creating an even crust. Set aside.
3. In a large mixing bowl, beat the cream cheese and sugar until smooth and creamy.
4. Add the eggs, one at a time, beating well after each addition. Stir in the vanilla extract.

5. Fold in the sour cream and rainbow sprinkles, being careful not to overmix.
6. Pour the cheesecake batter into the prepared crust, spreading it evenly.
7. Bake in the preheated oven for 55-60 minutes or until the edges are set but the center still has a slight jiggle.
8. Turn off the oven and leave the cheesecake inside for an additional hour to gradually cool down.
9. Remove the cheesecake from the oven and let it cool completely before refrigerating for at least 4 hours or overnight.
10. Once chilled and set, remove the sides of the springform pan and transfer the cheesecake to a serving platter.
11. Decorate the top with additional rainbow sprinkles for a festive touch.

Funfetti Pie Variations and Crust Options

Funfetti Cookie Pie

Ingredients for Funfetti Cookie Pie:

- 1 ¼ cups all-purpose flour
- ½ teaspoon baking soda
- ¼ teaspoon salt
- ½ cup unsalted butter, softened
- ½ cup granulated sugar
- ¼ cup packed light brown sugar
- 1 large egg
- 1 teaspoon vanilla extract
- ½ cup rainbow sprinkles
- 1 cup white chocolate chips

Instructions:

1. Preheat your oven to 350°F (175°C). Grease a 9-inch pie dish.
2. In a medium-sized bowl, whisk together the flour, baking soda, and salt. Set aside.
3. In a large mixing bowl, cream the softened butter, granulated sugar, and brown sugar until light and fluffy.
4. Beat in the egg and vanilla extract until well combined.
5. Gradually add the dry ingredients to the butter mixture, mixing until just combined.
6. Gently fold in the rainbow sprinkles and white chocolate chips.
7. Press the dough evenly into the greased pie dish, covering the bottom and sides.
8. Bake in the preheated oven for 25-30 minutes or until the edges are golden brown.
9. Remove the pie from the oven and let it cool completely before

slicing and serving.

Tips for Achieving a Perfect Texture

Room temperature ingredients: Ensure that your cream cheese, eggs, and sour cream (if using) are at room temperature before making the Funfetti cheesecake. This helps achieve a smoother texture and prevents lumps in the batter.

Avoid overmixing: When combining the cheesecake ingredients, mix until just combined. Overmixing can lead to a dense and heavy texture. Fold in the rainbow sprinkles gently to avoid overmixing them into the batter.

Gradual cooling: After baking, allow the cheesecake to cool gradually in the turned-off oven for an hour. This prevents sudden temperature changes and helps prevent cracking.

Chill thoroughly: To achieve the perfect texture, refrigerate the cheesecake for at least 4 hours or overnight before serving. This allows the flavors to develop and the cheesecake to firm up.

Prebaking pie crust: If making a Funfetti pie, prebake the crust before adding the filling. This helps ensure a crisp and stable crust, especially when using cookie dough or graham cracker crusts.

Keep pie crust chilled: When working with pie crusts, keep them chilled until ready to use. This helps maintain the flakiness and prevents the crust from shrinking during baking.

Blind baking: For pies with custard-like fillings, consider blind baking the crust before adding the Funfetti filling. This involves partially baking the crust without the filling to ensure it remains crisp and fully cooked.

By following these tips and techniques, you'll be able to achieve the perfect texture in your Funfetti cheesecakes and pies. Whether you're indulging in the creamy richness of a cheesecake or savoring the comforting sweetness of a pie, the Funfetti twist will add an extra element of joy to these delightful desserts. Enjoy the decadence and share them with friends and family for a truly memorable treat.

Chapter 6: Funfetti for Special Occasions

In this chapter, we'll explore the world of Funfetti cakes for special occasions. Whether it's a birthday celebration, a wedding, or a festive holiday gathering, Funfetti cakes have the power to bring an extra touch of joy and celebration to the occasion. Discover ideas for Funfetti cakes that will make birthdays unforgettable, explore wedding-worthy Funfetti cake options, and get inspired by holiday-themed Funfetti creations.

Funfetti Cakes for Birthdays and Celebrations

Funfetti Surprise Cake:

Create an element of surprise by baking a Funfetti cake with a hidden filling or center. Cut out a section of the baked cake and fill it with colorful candies, sprinkles, or even a smaller cake. Once sliced, the hidden surprise will delight the birthday celebrant and guests.

Funfetti Smash Cake:

Perfect for first birthdays or smash cake photo shoots, a Funfetti smash cake is a small, individual cake that the birthday child can freely enjoy and "smash" with their hands. Decorate the cake with vibrant buttercream frosting and an abundance of rainbow sprinkles.

Funfetti Number or Letter Cakes:

Shape the Funfetti cake batter into numbers or letters corresponding to the age or initials of the person celebrating their birthday. Decorate the shapes with colorful frosting, piped decorations, and plenty of sprinkles.

Wedding-Worthy Funfetti Cake Ideas

Funfetti Layered Wedding Cake:

Create a stunning multi-tiered wedding cake with layers of Funfetti cake, alternating with layers of complementary flavors like vanilla or chocolate. Decorate the cake with elegant buttercream or fondant, and finish with a touch of shimmer or delicate sugar flowers.

Funfetti Cupcake Tower:

Instead of a traditional wedding cake, opt for a tower of Funfetti cupcakes. Arrange them on tiers or a cupcake stand, and decorate with intricate piping designs, edible pearls, or fondant toppers that match the wedding theme or colors.

Funfetti Cake Pops or Macarons:

Offer bite-sized Funfetti treats like cake pops or macarons as part of a dessert table or wedding favors. Decorate them in elegant designs, such as with gold or silver dust, and package them beautifully for guests to enjoy or take home as a sweet memento.

Holiday-Themed Funfetti Creations

Funfetti Christmas Tree Cake:

Bake a Funfetti cake in a cone-shaped mold or trim a regular cake into a triangular shape. Decorate with green-tinted buttercream frosting, and use colorful sprinkles and edible ornaments to create a festive Christmas tree design.

Funfetti Fourth of July Cake:

Create a patriotic-themed Funfetti cake by layering red, white, and blue Funfetti cake layers. Frost with white buttercream or cream cheese frosting, and adorn the top with a cascade of red, white, and blue sprinkles for a stunning Independence Day dessert.

Funfetti Halloween Cake:

Bake a Funfetti cake and decorate it with black or purple buttercream frosting. Use Halloween-themed sprinkles, candy eyes, and fondant decorations in the shape of bats, spiders, or pumpkins to create a spooky yet playful Halloween cake.

Let these ideas inspire you to create Funfetti cakes that are tailor-made for birthdays, weddings, and holiday celebrations. Adapt the designs and decorations to suit your personal style and the theme of the occasion. With Funfetti's inherent joy and vibrant colors, these special occasion cakes will undoubtedly become unforgettable centerpieces that bring smiles and excitement to everyone involved.

Chapter 7: Gluten-Free and Vegan Funfetti Cakes

In this chapter, we'll explore delicious Funfetti cake recipes tailored to specific dietary needs. Whether you're following a gluten-free or vegan lifestyle, these recipes will allow you to enjoy the delightful flavors and vibrant colors of Funfetti cakes. Discover gluten-free Funfetti recipes, eggless and dairy-free options, as well as ingredient substitutions to accommodate various dietary needs.

Delicious Gluten-Free Funfetti Recipes

Gluten-Free Funfetti Cake

Ingredients:

- 2 cups gluten-free all-purpose flour
- 1 ½ teaspoons baking powder
- ½ teaspoon baking soda
- ¼ teaspoon salt
- 1 cup unsalted butter or dairy-free margarine, at room temperature
- 1 ½ cups granulated sugar
- 4 large eggs or egg replacer (such as applesauce or flaxseed mixture)
- 1 teaspoon vanilla extract
- 1 cup buttermilk or dairy-free milk of choice
- ½ cup gluten-free rainbow sprinkles

Instructions:

1. Preheat your oven to 350°F (175°C). Grease and line two 9-inch round cake pans with parchment paper.
2. In a medium-sized bowl, whisk together the gluten-free flour, baking powder, baking soda, and salt. Set aside.
3. In a separate large mixing bowl, cream the butter and granulated sugar together using an electric mixer until light and fluffy. This should take about 3-4 minutes.
4. Add the eggs (or egg replacer) one at a time, beating well after each addition. Stir in the vanilla extract.
5. Gradually add the dry ingredients to the butter mixture, alternating with the buttermilk (or dairy-free milk). Begin and end with the dry ingredients, mixing just until combined after each addition.
6. Gently fold in the gluten-free rainbow sprinkles, being careful not to overmix and cause them to bleed too much into the batter.
7. Divide the batter evenly between the prepared cake pans, smoothing the tops with a spatula.
8. Bake in the preheated oven for 25-30 minutes or until a toothpick inserted into the center of the cakes comes out clean.
9. Remove the cakes from the oven and let them cool in the pans for 10 minutes. Then, transfer them to a wire rack to cool completely before frosting.

Eggless and Dairy-Free Funfetti Options

Eggless Funfetti Cake

Ingredients:

- 2 cups all-purpose flour
- 1 ½ teaspoons baking powder
- ½ teaspoon baking soda
- ¼ teaspoon salt
- 1 cup unsweetened applesauce
- 1 cup granulated sugar
- ½ cup vegetable oil
- 1 teaspoon vanilla extract
- 1 cup dairy-free milk of choice
- ½ cup rainbow sprinkles

Instructions:

1. Preheat your oven to 350°F (175°C). Grease and line two 9-inch round cake pans with parchment paper.
2. In a medium-sized bowl, whisk together the flour, baking powder, baking soda, and salt. Set aside.
3. In a large mixing bowl, whisk together the applesauce, granulated sugar, vegetable oil, and vanilla extract until well combined.
4. Gradually add the dry ingredients to the applesauce mixture, alternating with the dairy-free milk. Begin and end with the dry ingredients, mixing just until combined after each addition.
5. Gently fold in the rainbow sprinkles, being careful not to overmix and cause them to bleed too much into the batter.
6. Divide the batter evenly between the prepared cake pans, smoothing the tops with a spatula.

7. Bake in the preheated oven for 25-30 minutes or until a toothpick inserted into the center of the cakes comes out clean.
8. Remove the cakes from the oven and let them cool in the pans for 10 minutes. Then, transfer them to a wire rack to cool completely before frosting.

Ingredient Substitutions for Dietary Needs

Gluten-Free Flour: Use a gluten-free all-purpose flour blend that is specifically formulated for baking. Look for a blend that includes ingredients like rice flour, tapioca starch, and xanthan gum to help achieve a similar texture to regular flour.

Dairy-Free Milk: Substitute dairy-free milk, such as almond milk, soy milk, or oat milk, for the buttermilk or regular milk in the recipe. Make sure to choose a variety that is unsweetened and unflavored.

Butter Substitutes: Replace butter with a dairy-free margarine or vegetable oil spread that is suitable for baking. Look for a brand that is specifically labeled as vegan or dairy-free.

Egg Replacers: Use suitable egg replacers like unsweetened applesauce, mashed bananas, or a flaxseed mixture (1 tablespoon ground flaxseed mixed with 3 tablespoons water) in place of eggs. These options work well as binders and moisture providers in Funfetti cakes.

With these gluten-free and vegan adaptations, you can enjoy the delightful flavors and colors of Funfetti cakes while adhering to your dietary needs. Make sure to read labels carefully to ensure that all ingredients, including sprinkles, are gluten-free and vegan. Enjoy these delicious treats without compromising on taste or celebration!

Chapter 8: Funfetti Dessert Mashups

In this chapter, we'll explore Funfetti dessert mashups that combine the joyous flavors of Funfetti with other delightful treats. From ice cream cakes and sundaes to cookies and bars, as well as indulgent milkshakes and parfaits, these mashups offer a creative twist on the classic Funfetti flavors. Get ready to enjoy the fusion of Funfetti with other beloved desserts in these deliciously delightful creations.

Funfetti Ice Cream Cake and Sundaes

Funfetti Ice Cream Cake

Ingredients:

- 1 Funfetti cake (you can use the Classic Funfetti Cake recipe from Chapter 2)
- 1.5 quarts of Funfetti ice cream
- Whipped cream, for garnish
- Rainbow sprinkles, for decoration

Instructions:

1. Bake the Funfetti cake according to the recipe in Chapter 2 and let it cool completely.
2. Once cooled, slice the Funfetti cake horizontally into two or three even layers.
3. In a 9-inch springform pan or cake pan, place one layer of Funfetti cake at the bottom.
4. Spread a layer of Funfetti ice cream on top of the cake layer, smoothing it out with a spatula.
5. Repeat the process, alternating layers of Funfetti cake and

Funfetti ice cream, until all the cake layers and ice cream are used. End with a layer of Funfetti ice cream on top.

6. Cover the pan with plastic wrap and freeze for at least 4 hours or until the ice cream is firm.

7. When ready to serve, remove the cake from the pan and place it on a serving platter.

8. Garnish the Funfetti ice cream cake with whipped cream and a generous sprinkle of rainbow sprinkles.

9. Slice and serve the Funfetti ice cream cake, enjoying the combination of cake, ice cream, and rainbow sprinkles in each delightful bite.

Funfetti Sundaes

Create a Funfetti-inspired sundae bar by setting out bowls of Funfetti ice cream, whipped cream, rainbow sprinkles, chocolate sauce, and any other desired toppings. Allow everyone to customize their sundaes by adding their favorite Funfetti treats like Funfetti cookies, crumbled Funfetti cake, or even a sprinkle of edible glitter.

Funfetti Cookies and Bars

Funfetti Cookies

Ingredients:

- 1 cup unsalted butter, softened
- 1 cup granulated sugar
- 1 cup packed light brown sugar
- 2 large eggs
- 1 teaspoon vanilla extract
- 3 cups all-purpose flour
- 1 teaspoon baking soda
- ½ teaspoon salt
- ½ cup rainbow sprinkles

Instructions:

1. Preheat your oven to 350°F (175°C) and line baking sheets with parchment paper.
2. In a large mixing bowl, cream together the softened butter, granulated sugar, and brown sugar until light and fluffy.
3. Add the eggs one at a time, beating well after each addition. Stir in the vanilla extract.
4. In a separate bowl, whisk together the flour, baking soda, and salt.
5. Gradually add the dry ingredients to the butter mixture, mixing until just combined.
6. Gently fold in the rainbow sprinkles.
7. Drop rounded tablespoons of dough onto the prepared baking sheets, spacing them about 2 inches apart.
8. Bake in the preheated oven for 10-12 minutes or until the edges are golden brown.

9. Remove the cookies from the oven and let them cool on the baking sheets for a few minutes before transferring them to a wire rack to cool completely.

Funfetti Bars

Transform the Funfetti cookie dough into bars by pressing the dough evenly into a greased 9x13-inch baking pan. Bake at 350°F (175°C) for 20-25 minutes or until the edges are golden brown. Let the bars cool completely before slicing into squares.

Funfetti-Inspired Milkshakes and Parfaits

Funfetti Milkshake

Ingredients:

- 2 cups vanilla ice cream
- 1 cup milk (dairy or non-dairy)
- ¼ cup rainbow sprinkles
- Whipped cream, for topping
- Rainbow sprinkles, for garnish

Instructions:

In a blender, combine the vanilla ice cream, milk, and rainbow sprinkles.

1. Blend until smooth and well combined.
2. Pour the Funfetti milkshake into a glass.
3. Top with whipped cream and a sprinkle of rainbow sprinkles.
4. Serve immediately and enjoy the delightful Funfetti flavors in milkshake form.

Funfetti Parfait

Create a Funfetti-inspired parfait by layering vanilla yogurt, crumbled Funfetti cookies, and fresh berries or other desired fruit in a glass or jar. Repeat the layers until the glass or jar is filled. Top with a dollop of whipped cream and a sprinkle of rainbow sprinkles for a fun and colorful treat.

These Funfetti dessert mashups offer a creative twist on the classic Funfetti flavors, allowing you to enjoy the delightful combination of cake, ice cream, cookies, and more. Whether you choose to make an ice cream cake, cookies, milkshakes, or parfaits, these mashups are sure to bring a smile to your face and a burst of joy to your taste buds. Enjoy these delightful treats on special occasions or whenever you're in the mood for a sweet and colorful indulgence.

Chapter 9: Funfetti for Kids and Family

In this chapter, we'll explore Funfetti cakes, activities, baking, and edible crafts that are perfect for kids and family fun. Funfetti is an ideal way to engage children in the kitchen and spark their creativity. From baking and decorating Funfetti cakes together to creating edible Funfetti crafts, these ideas are sure to create lasting memories and delicious treats for the whole family to enjoy.

Funfetti Cakes and Activities for Kids

Mini Funfetti Cupcakes:

Bake mini Funfetti cupcakes using a mini cupcake tin. Let the kids help measure and mix the ingredients. Once baked and cooled, let them decorate the cupcakes with their favorite frosting and rainbow sprinkles. Mini cupcakes are perfect for little hands and allow kids to have their own bite-sized treats.

Funfetti Cake Decorating Contest:

Set up a friendly cake decorating contest with the family. Provide pre-baked Funfetti cakes and a variety of frosting colors, sprinkles, and edible decorations. Each family member can decorate their own section of the cake, and once everyone is finished, vote for the most creative design. This activity allows for creativity, friendly competition, and lots of laughter.

Funfetti Cake Pops with Decorations:

Make Funfetti cake pops with the kids and let them decorate their own cake pops with colorful candy melts, sprinkles, and edible markers. Show them how to shape the cake pops and dip them in melted candy coating.

Then, let their imagination run wild as they decorate each cake pop to their heart's desire. It's a fun and interactive activity that results in tasty and adorable treats.

Funfetti Baking with the Family

Funfetti Pancakes:

Start the day with a fun-filled breakfast by making Funfetti pancakes. Simply add rainbow sprinkles to your favorite pancake batter and cook them on a griddle. Let the kids help mix the batter and sprinkle in the colorful additions. Serve the pancakes with a drizzle of maple syrup and extra sprinkles for a delightful morning treat.

Family Funfetti Cookie Baking:

Gather the family in the kitchen to bake Funfetti cookies together. Assign tasks to each family member, from measuring ingredients to mixing the dough and rolling it into balls. Let everyone take turns placing the dough balls on baking sheets and flattening them slightly. Bake the cookies and enjoy the delicious aroma that fills the kitchen. It's a wonderful opportunity for quality time and teamwork.

Funfetti Waffle Ice Cream Sandwiches:

Combine two beloved treats by making Funfetti waffles and using them as a base for ice cream sandwiches. Prepare Funfetti waffle batter and cook them in a waffle maker. Once cooled, sandwich a scoop of your favorite ice cream between two Funfetti waffles. Roll the edges in rainbow sprinkles for an extra festive touch. This treat is sure to delight both kids and adults.

Edible Funfetti Crafts and Creations

Funfetti Edible Playdough:

Make edible Funfetti playdough with the kids using a simple recipe that combines flour, salt, oil, cream of tartar, and rainbow sprinkles. Let them mix and knead the dough until it reaches a playdough consistency. Encourage creativity by providing cookie cutters, rolling pins, and other tools for them to shape and mold their edible creations.

Funfetti Rice Krispie Treats:

Put a Funfetti twist on a classic treat by making Funfetti Rice Krispie treats. Prepare the Rice Krispie mixture as usual, but add rainbow sprinkles to the melted marshmallow mixture before combining with the cereal. Press the mixture into a greased baking dish, let it set, and cut into squares. The colorful sprinkles add a playful touch to this nostalgic treat.

Funfetti Popcorn Balls:

Combine popcorn, melted marshmallows, and rainbow sprinkles to create Funfetti popcorn balls. Let the kids help stir the popcorn into the marshmallow mixture and add the sprinkles. Once mixed, shape the mixture into balls and let them cool and set. These fun and tasty treats are perfect for snacking or as party favors for special occasions.

These Funfetti cakes, activities, baking, and edible crafts provide endless fun for kids and families. Whether it's a weekend baking session, a friendly cake decorating contest, or creating edible crafts, the joy of Funfetti and the involvement of the whole family make these moments truly special. Embrace the creativity and deliciousness of Funfetti, and let the memories unfold as you bond and have fun together in the kitchen.

Chapter 10: Funfetti for Breakfast and Brunch

In this chapter, we'll explore Funfetti-inspired breakfast and brunch ideas that are perfect for starting the day with a touch of joy and celebration. From fluffy pancakes and crispy waffles to delectable French toast and muffins, as well as delightful breakfast pastries, these Funfetti creations will make your mornings extra special.

Funfetti Pancakes and Waffles

Funfetti Pancakes

Ingredients:

- 2 cups all-purpose flour
- 2 tablespoons granulated sugar
- 2 teaspoons baking powder
- ½ teaspoon baking soda
- ½ teaspoon salt
- 2 cups buttermilk
- 2 large eggs
- ¼ cup unsalted butter, melted
- ½ cup rainbow sprinkles

Instructions:

1. In a large mixing bowl, whisk together the flour, sugar, baking powder, baking soda, and salt.
2. In a separate bowl, whisk together the buttermilk, eggs, and melted butter.
3. Pour the wet ingredients into the dry ingredients and stir until just combined. Be careful not to overmix; a few lumps are okay.

4. Gently fold in the rainbow sprinkles.
5. Preheat a griddle or non-stick skillet over medium heat and lightly grease it.
6. Pour ¼ cup of batter onto the griddle for each pancake. Cook until bubbles form on the surface, then flip and cook for an additional 1-2 minutes, or until golden brown.
7. Repeat with the remaining batter, adding more butter or oil as needed.
8. Serve the Funfetti pancakes warm with maple syrup and extra rainbow sprinkles on top.

Funfetti Waffles

Ingredients:

- 2 cups all-purpose flour
- ¼ cup granulated sugar
- 2 teaspoons baking powder
- ½ teaspoon baking soda
- ½ teaspoon salt
- 2 cups buttermilk
- 2 large eggs
- ½ cup unsalted butter, melted
- ½ cup rainbow sprinkles

Instructions:

1. In a large mixing bowl, whisk together the flour, sugar, baking powder, baking soda, and salt.
2. In a separate bowl, whisk together the buttermilk, eggs, and melted butter.
3. Pour the wet ingredients into the dry ingredients and stir until just combined. Be careful not to overmix; a few lumps are okay.
4. Gently fold in the rainbow sprinkles.
5. Preheat a waffle iron according to the manufacturer's instructions.
6. Pour the batter onto the preheated waffle iron and cook until golden brown and crisp.
7. Repeat with the remaining batter, greasing the waffle iron as needed.
8. Serve the Funfetti waffles warm with maple syrup and a sprinkle of rainbow sprinkles.

Funfetti French Toast and Muffins

Funfetti French Toast

Ingredients:

- 8 slices of bread (preferably brioche or challah)
- 4 large eggs
- ½ cup milk
- 1 teaspoon vanilla extract
- ¼ cup rainbow sprinkles
- Butter or cooking spray, for greasing the pan

Instructions:

1. In a shallow bowl, whisk together the eggs, milk, and vanilla extract.
2. Place the rainbow sprinkles in a separate shallow bowl.
3. Dip each slice of bread into the egg mixture, allowing it to soak for a few seconds on each side.
4. Transfer the soaked bread to the bowl of rainbow sprinkles, pressing gently to adhere the sprinkles to both sides of the bread.
5. Preheat a large skillet or griddle over medium heat and grease it with butter or cooking spray.
6. Place the coated bread slices onto the hot skillet and cook for 2-3 minutes on each side, or until golden brown.
7. Repeat with the remaining bread slices.
8. Serve the Funfetti French toast warm with maple syrup and a sprinkle of extra rainbow sprinkles, if desired.

Funfetti Muffins

Ingredients:

- 2 cups all-purpose flour
- ½ cup granulated sugar
- 2 teaspoons baking powder
- ½ teaspoon baking soda
- ½ teaspoon salt
- ¾ cup buttermilk
- ½ cup unsalted butter, melted
- 2 large eggs
- 1 teaspoon vanilla extract
- ½ cup rainbow sprinkles

Instructions:

1. Preheat your oven to 375°F (190°C) and line a muffin tin with paper liners.
2. In a large mixing bowl, whisk together the flour, sugar, baking powder, baking soda, and salt.
3. In a separate bowl, whisk together the buttermilk, melted butter, eggs, and vanilla extract.
4. Pour the wet ingredients into the dry ingredients and stir until just combined. Be careful not to overmix; a few lumps are okay.
5. Gently fold in the rainbow sprinkles.
6. Divide the batter evenly among the prepared muffin cups, filling each about ¾ full.
7. Bake in the preheated oven for 15-18 minutes, or until a toothpick inserted into the center comes out clean.
8. Remove the muffins from the oven and let them cool in the tin for a few minutes before transferring them to a wire rack to cool completely.

Funfetti-Inspired Breakfast Pastries

Funfetti Cinnamon Rolls

Prepare your favorite cinnamon roll dough or use pre-made dough. Roll out the dough into a rectangle and sprinkle rainbow sprinkles and cinnamon-sugar mixture over the surface. Roll up the dough tightly, slice it into individual rolls, and place them in a greased baking dish. Allow them to rise according to the dough recipe instructions, then bake until golden brown. Drizzle with cream cheese frosting and extra rainbow sprinkles.

Funfetti Croissants

Use store-bought or homemade croissant dough. Roll out the dough and sprinkle rainbow sprinkles over the surface. Roll up the dough tightly into croissant shapes and bake according to the dough recipe instructions until golden and flaky. These Funfetti croissants are a delightful twist on the classic breakfast pastry.

Funfetti Danish Pastries

Make or purchase puff pastry dough. Cut the dough into squares or rectangles and place a spoonful of rainbow sprinkles in the center of each piece. Fold the corners of the dough towards the center to create a seal and form a well in the middle. Fill the well with cream cheese or fruit preserves. Bake according to the puff pastry recipe instructions until golden and puffed. Drizzle with a glaze and sprinkle with extra rainbow sprinkles.

These Funfetti breakfast and brunch ideas are sure to bring a smile to your face and make your mornings extra special. Whether you choose fluffy pancakes, crispy waffles, delectable French toast, delightful muffins, or fun-filled breakfast pastries, the addition of rainbow sprinkles adds a touch of joy to each bite. Enjoy these delightful treats with your loved ones and start your day off on a celebratory note.

Chapter 11: International Funfetti Flavors

In this chapter, we'll embark on a journey to explore Funfetti-inspired treats from around the world. Funfetti's vibrant colors and joyful flavors can be adapted to various cultural cuisines, creating unique and delightful fusion desserts. Discover international Funfetti flavors, explore Funfetti fusion desserts, and learn how to adapt Funfetti to different culinary traditions.

Exploring Funfetti-Inspired Treats from Around the World

Matcha Funfetti Cake (Japan):

Incorporate the flavors of Japan by adding matcha powder to a Funfetti cake batter. The earthy and vibrant green matcha complements the colorful sprinkles, creating a delightful fusion of Japanese and Funfetti flavors. Serve the cake with a dusting of matcha powder and a sprinkle of edible cherry blossoms for an extra touch of elegance.

Chai Funfetti Cookies (India):

Infuse the warm and aromatic flavors of chai into Funfetti cookies by adding a blend of chai spices like cardamom, cinnamon, ginger, and cloves. The combination of the familiar Funfetti sprinkles with the rich chai spices creates a unique and flavorful treat that pays homage to Indian culinary traditions.

Dulce de Leche Funfetti Cupcakes (Latin America):

Embrace the sweet and creamy flavors of Latin America by filling Funfetti cupcakes with dulce de leche. Once baked and cooled, hollow out the center of each cupcake and fill it with a spoonful of dulce de leche. Top the cupcakes with a swirl of dulce de leche buttercream frosting and a sprinkle of rainbow sprinkles.

Funfetti Fusion Desserts

Funfetti Macaron Ice Cream Sandwich (France and Italy):

Combine the elegance of French macarons with the indulgence of Italian gelato to create Funfetti macaron ice cream sandwiches. Use Funfetti-flavored macarons as the sandwich shells and fill them with a scoop of gelato in a complementary flavor. Roll the edges of the gelato in rainbow sprinkles for a touch of Funfetti flair.

Funfetti Mochi Cake (Hawaii and Japan):

Fuse the chewy texture of Hawaiian mochi with Funfetti flavors to create a unique Funfetti mochi cake. Make a traditional mochi cake base, but incorporate rainbow sprinkles into the batter. The result is a delightful combination of the soft and chewy mochi texture with the vibrant colors and flavors of Funfetti.

Funfetti Churro Bites (Spain and Latin America):

Put a Funfetti twist on the beloved Spanish and Latin American treat by creating Funfetti churro bites. Fry churro dough until golden and crispy, then toss the warm churros in a mixture of sugar and rainbow sprinkles. Serve them with a side of chocolate dipping sauce for a Funfetti-infused twist on this classic dessert.

Adapting Funfetti Flavors to Different Cultures

When adapting Funfetti flavors to different cultures, consider incorporating local ingredients, spices, or flavors that are popular in that particular cuisine. Here are a few examples:

Funfetti Baklava (Middle East):

Infuse the classic Middle Eastern dessert with Funfetti flavors by adding rainbow sprinkles and a touch of rosewater or orange blossom water to the baklava filling. The result is a playful and delightful twist on this traditional pastry.

Funfetti Tres Leches Cake (Mexico):

Create a Funfetti version of the beloved Mexican dessert by baking a Funfetti cake and soaking it with a mixture of three milks (evaporated milk, condensed milk, and heavy cream). Top the cake with whipped cream and a sprinkle of rainbow sprinkles for an extra festive touch.

Funfetti Pão de Queijo (Brazil):

Give the Brazilian cheese bread a Funfetti makeover by adding rainbow sprinkles to the dough before baking. The combination of the cheesy bread with the colorful sprinkles creates a delightful contrast of flavors and textures.

Remember to be creative and experiment with different flavor combinations that reflect the culinary traditions and ingredients of the culture you're drawing inspiration from. Have fun infusing Funfetti flavors into international treats and let your taste buds explore the delightful fusion of cultures.

Chapter 12: Boozy Funfetti Treats

In this chapter, we'll dive into the world of boozy Funfetti treats. These delightful creations combine the joyful flavors of Funfetti with a touch of alcohol, making them perfect for adults who want to indulge in some playful and spirited treats. Explore Funfetti-infused cocktails and mocktails, discover Funfetti-spiked desserts, and learn tips for incorporating alcohol into Funfetti recipes.

Funfetti-Infused Cocktails and Mocktails

Funfetti Cake Martini:

Shake up a playful and sweet Funfetti Cake Martini by combining cake-flavored vodka, amaretto liqueur, white chocolate liqueur, and a splash of cream. Rim the martini glass with rainbow sprinkles for an extra festive touch. Garnish with a Funfetti cake bite or a skewer of rainbow sprinkles.

Funfetti Mimosa:

Add a colorful twist to your brunch routine with a Funfetti Mimosa. Mix orange juice, champagne, and a splash of cake-flavored vodka. Serve in champagne flutes and garnish with a sprinkle-coated orange slice. The combination of citrusy flavors and the touch of Funfetti will make any brunch feel extra special.

Funfetti Sparkling Lemonade (Mocktail):

Create a refreshing and non-alcoholic Funfetti mocktail by combining sparkling lemonade, a splash of grenadine syrup, and a handful of rainbow sprinkles. Serve it in a tall glass filled with ice and garnish with a lemon slice and a sprinkle-coated rim.

Funfetti-Spiked Desserts for Adults

Funfetti White Russian:

Give the classic White Russian cocktail a Funfetti twist. Combine vodka, coffee liqueur, cream, and a splash of cake-flavored vodka. Shake or stir well and serve over ice in a rocks glass. Garnish with whipped cream and rainbow sprinkles for a playful presentation.

Boozy Funfetti Ice Cream:

Make homemade Funfetti ice cream with a boozy twist by adding a splash of your favorite liqueur, such as vanilla vodka or amaretto, to the ice cream base during the churning process. The alcohol will enhance the flavors and create a delightful adult version of this beloved frozen treat.

Funfetti Bread Pudding with Bourbon Sauce:

Create a decadent Funfetti bread pudding by soaking cubes of Funfetti cake in a mixture of eggs, milk, sugar, and a splash of bourbon. Bake the bread pudding until golden and set. Serve it warm with a drizzle of bourbon-infused caramel sauce for a boozy and indulgent dessert.

Tips for Incorporating Alcohol into Funfetti Recipes

Choose complementary flavors: Select liqueurs or spirits that complement the flavors of Funfetti. Vanilla, almond, chocolate, and coffee liqueurs are excellent choices that pair well with the sweet and playful nature of Funfetti.

Start with small amounts: When incorporating alcohol into Funfetti recipes, start with smaller amounts and adjust to taste. Too much alcohol can overpower the flavors and alter the texture of the baked goods. It's best to add a little at a time and taste as you go.

Substituting alcohol in recipes: If you prefer to avoid alcohol or make mocktail versions of the boozy treats, consider using alcohol-free extracts or flavorings that mimic the taste of specific liqueurs or spirits. These can be found in specialty baking stores or online.

Incorporate alcohol during assembly or baking: Depending on the recipe, you can incorporate alcohol by adding it directly to the batter or dough, brushing it on the cake layers, drizzling it over the finished dessert, or infusing it into creams, sauces, or glazes.

Alcohol in frostings and fillings: For frostings or fillings, such as buttercream or cream cheese frosting, you can add a small amount of alcohol, like flavored liqueur or extracts, to enhance the flavors. However, be mindful of the consistency and adjust the amount of liquid accordingly.

Remember to enjoy boozy Funfetti treats responsibly and be aware of the alcohol content in each recipe. These treats are designed for adult indulgence and can add an extra layer of fun and sophistication to your Funfetti experience. Cheers to playful flavors and delightful moments!

Chapter 13: Healthier Funfetti Alternatives

In this chapter, we'll explore healthier alternatives for Funfetti treats. These recipes aim to reduce sugar content, incorporate nutritious ingredient substitutions, and create Funfetti-inspired treats with added health benefits. Enjoy the playful flavors of Funfetti while making choices that align with your dietary preferences and goals.

Funfetti Recipes with Reduced Sugar

Reduced-Sugar Funfetti Cake:

Create a Funfetti cake with reduced sugar content by using a combination of granulated sugar and a sugar substitute like stevia or erythritol. You can also reduce the overall amount of sugar called for in the recipe. The colorful sprinkles will still add sweetness and joy to the cake, even with less sugar.

Low-Sugar Funfetti Cookies:

Make Funfetti cookies with reduced sugar by using a combination of granulated sugar and a sugar substitute like monk fruit sweetener or coconut sugar. The rainbow sprinkles will provide bursts of sweetness, allowing you to cut back on the overall sugar content while still enjoying the playful Funfetti flavors.

Nutritious Ingredient Substitutions

Whole Wheat Funfetti Pancakes:

Swap all-purpose flour with whole wheat flour to create whole grain Funfetti pancakes. The whole wheat flour adds fiber and nutrients to the pancakes, making them a healthier choice. You can also reduce the sugar content by using a sugar substitute or cutting back on the amount of sugar used in the batter.

Greek Yogurt Funfetti Dip:

Create a healthier Funfetti dip by using Greek yogurt as the base. Mix Greek yogurt with a small amount of sweetener, such as honey or maple syrup, and fold in rainbow sprinkles. Serve the dip with fruit slices or whole grain crackers for a nutritious and colorful snack.

Funfetti-Inspired Treats with Added Health Benefits

Funfetti Protein Balls:

Make protein balls with a Funfetti twist by combining protein powder, nut butter, oats, honey or maple syrup, and rainbow sprinkles. Roll the mixture into bite-sized balls and refrigerate until firm. These protein-packed treats provide a boost of energy and satisfy your Funfetti cravings in a healthier way.

Veggie Funfetti Muffins:

Create colorful and nutritious Funfetti muffins by adding finely grated vegetables like carrots or zucchini to the batter. The vegetables add moisture, fiber, and vitamins to the muffins, making them a wholesome choice. Use a combination of whole wheat flour and all-purpose flour for added nutrients.

Funfetti Chia Pudding:

Prepare a Funfetti chia pudding by combining chia seeds, milk (dairy or plant-based), a small amount of sweetener, and rainbow sprinkles. Let the mixture sit in the refrigerator overnight until it thickens. Chia seeds are rich in fiber, omega-3 fatty acids, and antioxidants, making this a nutritious and satisfying Funfetti-inspired treat.

Remember, while these alternatives offer healthier options compared to traditional Funfetti treats, moderation is still key. Enjoy these treats as part of a balanced diet and consider portion sizes that align with your dietary goals. By making small changes and incorporating nutritious ingredients, you can still indulge in the playful flavors of Funfetti while nourishing your body.

Chapter 14: Funfetti Cakes for Seasonal Delights

In this chapter, we'll explore Funfetti cakes and treats inspired by the seasons. From spring-themed delights bursting with floral flavors to summer-inspired treats that celebrate the sunniest time of the year, as well as festive creations that embrace the colors and flavors of fall and winter, these Funfetti cakes will bring seasonal joy to your celebrations.

Spring-Themed Funfetti Cakes

Lemon Blossom Funfetti Cake:

Create a spring-inspired Funfetti cake by infusing the batter with lemon zest and a splash of lemon juice. Add a layer of lemon curd between the cake layers for a burst of citrus flavor. Decorate the cake with pastel-colored frosting, edible flowers, and delicate sprinkles for a beautiful and refreshing springtime treat.

Strawberry Shortcake Funfetti Cake:

Celebrate the arrival of juicy strawberries by incorporating them into a Funfetti cake. Add diced fresh strawberries to the cake batter and fill the layers with whipped cream and sliced strawberries. Garnish the cake with additional fresh berries and a sprinkle of rainbow sprinkles. It's a delightful way to embrace the flavors of spring.

Summer-Inspired Funfetti Treats

Piña Colada Funfetti Cupcakes:

Transport yourself to a tropical paradise with Piña Colada Funfetti cupcakes. Infuse the cake batter with pineapple juice and coconut extract. Fill the cupcakes with pineapple compote and top them with coconut-flavored frosting. Garnish with toasted coconut flakes and a pineapple wedge for a taste of summer in every bite.

Watermelon Funfetti Cake:

Create a watermelon-themed Funfetti cake by coloring the batter with vibrant green and pink hues. Stack the cake layers to resemble a watermelon and frost it with green buttercream. Add mini chocolate chips as "seeds" and decorate the cake with a watermelon rind pattern using a piping bag. It's a playful and refreshing treat for hot summer days.

Festive Funfetti Creations for Fall and Winter

Pumpkin Spice Funfetti Bundt Cake:

Embrace the flavors of fall by adding pumpkin puree and warm spices like cinnamon, nutmeg, and cloves to a Funfetti bundt cake. The result is a moist and flavorful cake that perfectly captures the essence of autumn. Dust the cake with powdered sugar and serve it with a dollop of whipped cream for a cozy and festive treat.

Peppermint Mocha Funfetti Cookies:

Celebrate the holiday season with Peppermint Mocha Funfetti cookies. Add cocoa powder, crushed candy canes, and a hint of peppermint extract to the cookie dough. Mix in the Funfetti sprinkles for a colorful twist. These cookies are the perfect blend of chocolate, mint, and holiday cheer.

These seasonal Funfetti cakes and treats add a touch of whimsy and joy to your celebrations throughout the year. Whether you're embracing the freshness of spring, basking in the sun of summer, or immersing yourself in the festive spirit of fall and winter, these Funfetti creations will delight your taste buds and bring a smile to everyone's faces.

Chapter 15: Quick and Easy Funfetti Fixes

In this chapter, we'll explore quick and easy Funfetti fixes for those times when you're craving a delicious treat but are short on time. These recipes require minimal preparation and are perfect for satisfying your Funfetti cravings in a hurry. From mug cakes that can be whipped up in minutes to no-bake desserts and shortcut Funfetti hacks, these recipes are your go-to solutions for quick and delightful Funfetti fixes.

Simple and Speedy Funfetti Mug Cakes

Funfetti Mug Cake (Single Serving):

Ingredients:

- 4 tablespoons all-purpose flour
- 2 tablespoons granulated sugar
- 1/4 teaspoon baking powder
- Pinch of salt
- 3 tablespoons milk
- 1 tablespoon vegetable oil
- 1/4 teaspoon vanilla extract
- 1 tablespoon rainbow sprinkles

Instructions:

1. In a microwave-safe mug, whisk together the flour, sugar, baking powder, and salt.
2. Add the milk, vegetable oil, and vanilla extract to the mug. Stir until the batter is smooth and well combined.

3. Fold in the rainbow sprinkles, reserving a few for garnish.
4. Microwave the mug on high for approximately 1 minute and 30 seconds, or until the cake has risen and is set in the center.
5. Allow the mug cake to cool for a minute or two before enjoying. Top with additional rainbow sprinkles, if desired.

No-Bake Funfetti Desserts

Funfetti Cheesecake Bars:

Ingredients:

- 2 cups crushed graham crackers
- 1/2 cup unsalted butter, melted
- 16 oz cream cheese, softened
- 1/2 cup powdered sugar
- 1 teaspoon vanilla extract
- 1 cup rainbow sprinkles

Instructions:

1. In a mixing bowl, combine the crushed graham crackers and melted butter. Press the mixture into the bottom of a greased 9x9-inch baking dish to form the crust.
2. In a separate bowl, beat the cream cheese until smooth and creamy. Add the powdered sugar and vanilla extract, and continue to beat until well combined.
3. Fold in the rainbow sprinkles, reserving a few for sprinkling on top.
4. Spread the cream cheese mixture evenly over the crust in the baking dish.
5. Refrigerate the Funfetti cheesecake bars for at least 2 hours, or until firm.
6. Cut into squares and serve chilled. Garnish with the reserved rainbow sprinkles.

Shortcut Funfetti Hacks for Busy Bakers

Funfetti Cake Mix Cookies:

Ingredients:

- 1 box Funfetti cake mix
- 1/2 cup vegetable oil
- 2 large eggs
- 1/4 cup rainbow sprinkles

Instructions:

1. Preheat your oven to the temperature indicated on the cake mix box.
2. In a mixing bowl, combine the Funfetti cake mix, vegetable oil, and eggs. Stir until the ingredients are well combined.
3. Fold in the rainbow sprinkles, reserving a few for pressing on top of the cookie dough.
4. Drop rounded tablespoons of dough onto a greased or lined baking sheet, spacing them about 2 inches apart.
5. Gently press a few rainbow sprinkles onto the top of each cookie.
6. Bake the cookies according to the package instructions, or until the edges are golden brown.
7. Allow the cookies to cool on the baking sheet for a few minutes before transferring them to a wire rack to cool completely.

These quick and easy Funfetti fixes are perfect for when you're craving a delightful treat but don't have much time to spare. Whether you're making a single-serving mug cake, a no-bake cheesecake bar, or using a shortcut with cake mix cookies, these recipes will satisfy your Funfetti cravings without the need for extensive preparation or baking time. Enjoy the fun and deliciousness of Funfetti in a flash!

Chapter 16: Funfetti Cake Decoration Techniques

In this chapter, we'll explore the art of Funfetti cake decorating. From mastering the basics to advanced decoration ideas and designs, these techniques will help you create stunning Funfetti masterpieces. Discover tips for achieving professional-looking cakes, learn advanced decorating techniques, and find inspiration for adding a personal touch to your Funfetti creations.

Mastering Funfetti Cake Decorating Basics

Leveling and Layering:

Start by leveling your Funfetti cake layers to ensure a smooth and even surface. Use a serrated knife or a cake leveler to trim off any domed tops. When layering the cake, apply a thin layer of frosting between each layer to create stability and enhance the taste.

Crumb Coat:

Apply a thin layer of frosting, called a crumb coat, to seal in the crumbs and provide a smooth foundation for the final layer of frosting. Use a bench scraper or an offset spatula to spread a thin layer of frosting around the sides and top of the cake. Refrigerate the cake for a short time to allow the crumb coat to set before applying the final layer of frosting.

Frosting Techniques:

Experiment with different frosting techniques to achieve various textures and designs. You can try classic techniques like smooth buttercream, textured buttercream, or piped rosettes. You can also explore using a palette knife for a rustic look or using a piping bag with different tips to create patterns and borders.

Advanced Decorating Ideas and Designs

Funfetti Drip Cake:

Create a show-stopping Funfetti drip cake by covering the cake with a thick layer of buttercream frosting and allowing it to set. Then, melt white or colored candy melts and pour them over the top of the cake, allowing the drips to flow down the sides. Finish by adding additional decorations such as macarons, edible flowers, or sprinkles on top.

Ombré Funfetti Cake:

Achieve a beautiful ombré effect by using different shades of Funfetti batter or tinting white batter with gel food coloring. Bake multiple layers of cake with varying shades, from light to dark. Stack the layers, starting with the lightest shade at the bottom. Frost the cake with a complementary-colored buttercream and smooth the sides for a stunning gradient effect.

Funfetti Floral Cake:

Transform your Funfetti cake into a floral masterpiece by piping buttercream flowers on the surface. Use different piping tips to create various flower shapes, such as roses, daisies, or hydrangeas. Add colorful sprinkles as the flower centers for an extra pop of Funfetti flair.

Tips for Creating Personalized Funfetti Masterpieces

Custom Sprinkle Blends:

Create your own unique sprinkle blends by combining different types and colors of sprinkles. Mix in edible glitter, metallic pearls, or even tiny edible sugar shapes for a personalized touch. These custom blends can be used to decorate the cake's exterior or to sprinkle between the layers for added fun and flavor.

Personalized Cake Toppers:

Design and create personalized cake toppers that reflect the occasion or the recipient's interests. You can use fondant or gum paste to shape initials, names, or decorative elements. Alternatively, print out and cut personalized messages or images on edible paper using food-safe ink and place them on top of the cake.

Funfetti Surprise Inside:

Add an element of surprise to your Funfetti cake by incorporating a hidden design or pattern inside the cake. Using a round cookie cutter or a stencil, cut out a shape from each layer before assembling the cake. Fill the cut-out sections with different colored Funfetti or even a contrasting flavor of cake. When the cake is sliced, the hidden design will be revealed.

Remember to have fun and experiment with different decorating techniques. Don't be afraid to get creative and let your imagination run wild. Whether you're mastering the basics, trying advanced designs, or personalizing your Funfetti creations, these tips will help you create stunning and personalized Funfetti cakes that are as delightful to look at as they are to eat.

Chapter 17: Funfetti Cakes Around the World

In this chapter, we'll embark on a global journey to discover Funfetti cakes in different cultures. From unique Funfetti variations to exploring Funfetti-inspired traditions, we'll delve into the colorful and joyful world of Funfetti cakes around the globe.

Funfetti Cakes in Different Cultures

Funfetti Bolo de Festa (Brazil):

In Brazil, Funfetti cakes, known as "Bolo de Festa," are popular for celebrating birthdays and special occasions. These cakes often feature colorful layers, filled with Brigadeiro (a chocolate truffle-like filling), and covered with a smooth and glossy chocolate ganache. The vibrant appearance and rich flavors make them a festive favorite.

Confetti Cake (United States):

The United States is known for its love of Funfetti cakes, commonly referred to as "Confetti Cake." These cakes feature a vanilla base with rainbow sprinkles mixed into the batter. They are often paired with a creamy vanilla buttercream frosting and topped with an abundance of additional rainbow sprinkles.

Unique Funfetti Variations Globally

Piñata Funfetti Cake (Mexico):

In Mexico, a popular variation of Funfetti cake is the Piñata Cake. It's a hollow cake filled with candies or small treats. The cake is typically covered with colorful frosting and adorned with festive decorations. When sliced, the hidden treats spill out, creating a delightful surprise for the celebrants.

Rainbow Funfetti Cake (Australia):

In Australia, Funfetti cakes are often referred to as "Rainbow Cakes." These cakes feature layers of brightly colored cake batter, stacked with fillings such as buttercream or whipped cream. The exterior is typically covered with pastel-colored frosting, creating a whimsical and vibrant dessert.

Exploring Funfetti-Inspired Traditions

Holi Funfetti Cake (India):

Holi, the festival of colors celebrated in India, inspired Funfetti-like traditions. During Holi, people engage in joyful color fights by throwing vibrant colored powders at each other. This celebration has influenced Funfetti-inspired cakes and desserts that feature a burst of colorful flavors and decorations.

Sprinkle Cake (Netherlands):

In the Netherlands, a popular Funfetti-inspired tradition is the "Sprinkle Cake." This cake is typically served at children's birthday parties and features a simple sponge cake topped with a thick layer of buttercream frosting, covered in an array of colorful sprinkles. It's a festive treat that brings smiles to both young and old.

Funfetti Basbousa (Middle East):

Basbousa, a traditional Middle Eastern sweet cake, has been given a Funfetti twist. The cake is typically made with semolina, yogurt, and sugar syrup, and it's now common to find versions adorned with colorful sprinkles. The addition of sprinkles adds a playful touch to this already delightful Middle Eastern treat.

These Funfetti variations and traditions from around the world highlight the universal joy that colorful cakes bring to celebrations. Whether it's the indulgent Bolo de Festa in Brazil, the surprise-filled Piñata Cake in Mexico, or the vibrant Rainbow Cake in Australia, Funfetti cakes continue to spread happiness and create sweet memories across different cultures.

Chapter 18: Funfetti Cake Failures and Fixes

In this chapter, we'll address common Funfetti cake baking mistakes and provide troubleshooting solutions to turn your cake mishaps into delicious creations. We understand that baking doesn't always go as planned, but with a few adjustments and tips, you can overcome these challenges and still enjoy a delightful Funfetti cake.

Dense or Dry Funfetti Cake

Ingredients:

- 2 cups all-purpose flour
- 1 1/2 teaspoons baking powder
- 1/2 teaspoon baking soda
- 1/4 teaspoon salt
- 1/2 cup unsalted butter, softened
- 1 1/4 cups granulated sugar
- 3 large eggs
- 1 teaspoon vanilla extract
- 1 cup buttermilk
- 1/2 cup rainbow sprinkles

Instructions:

1. Preheat the oven to 350°F (175°C). Grease and flour two 9-inch round cake pans.
2. In a medium bowl, whisk together the flour, baking powder, baking soda, and salt. Set aside.
3. In a large mixing bowl, cream the butter and sugar together until light and fluffy. Add the eggs, one at a time, beating well after each addition. Stir in the vanilla extract.

4. Gradually add the dry ingredients to the butter mixture, alternating with the buttermilk. Begin and end with the dry ingredients, mixing until just combined. Avoid overmixing.
5. Gently fold in the rainbow sprinkles.
6. Divide the batter evenly between the prepared cake pans.
7. Bake for 25-30 minutes, or until a toothpick inserted into the center of the cakes comes out clean.
8. Remove the cakes from the oven and let them cool in the pans for 10 minutes. Then transfer them to a wire rack to cool completely.

Troubleshooting Solutions:

If your Funfetti cake turns out dense or dry, it may be due to overmixing the batter. When combining the dry ingredients with the wet ingredients, mix until just combined to avoid developing excess gluten, which can lead to a dense texture. Be gentle when folding in the sprinkles as well.

Another possible cause of dryness is overbaking the cake. Check for doneness a few minutes before the recommended baking time by inserting a toothpick into the center of the cake. If it comes out clean or with a few moist crumbs, it's ready to be removed from the oven.

To add moisture to a dry Funfetti cake, you can brush each layer with a simple syrup made from equal parts sugar and water. This will help to rehydrate the cake layers.

Transforming Cake Mishaps into Delicious Creations:

If your Funfetti cake turns out too dense to enjoy as a traditional cake, consider turning it into a trifle. Cut the cake into cubes, layer it with whipped cream or custard, and add fresh berries or other fruits for a delicious and visually appealing dessert.

Crumbled Funfetti cake can be transformed into cake pops. Mix the crumbled cake with a little frosting to create a dough-like consistency, roll into balls, and insert lollipop sticks. Dip the cake pops in melted chocolate and decorate with additional sprinkles.

Dry Funfetti cake layers can be repurposed into a delightful trifle or used as a base for ice cream cake. Layer the cake with ice cream, whipped cream, and your favorite toppings for a refreshing and indulgent dessert.

Remember, mistakes happen in the kitchen, and it's all part of the learning process. By understanding the common issues and their solutions, you can troubleshoot and transform cake failures into delicious and creative treats. Don't be afraid to experiment and have fun with your Funfetti cake mishaps!

Chapter 19: Funfetti Cake Gift Ideas

In this chapter, we'll explore homemade Funfetti gifts for special occasions, Funfetti-inspired packaging and presentation ideas, as well as DIY Funfetti cake mix jars and gift baskets. These thoughtful and delicious gifts will bring joy to your loved ones and make any celebration extra special.

Homemade Funfetti Gifts for Special Occasions

Funfetti Cake in a Jar:

Layer the dry ingredients of a Funfetti cake, including the flour, sugar, baking powder, and rainbow sprinkles, in a clean mason jar. Attach a tag with the remaining ingredients and baking instructions. Decorate the jar with a ribbon or personalized label. This gift allows the recipient to enjoy the fun of baking a homemade Funfetti cake at their convenience.

Funfetti Cupcake Bouquet:

Create a stunning bouquet of Funfetti cupcakes by arranging them in a flowerpot or decorative container. Use a variety of frosting colors and piping techniques to create different "flower" designs on the cupcakes. Arrange them with colorful tissue paper or artificial flowers to resemble a bouquet. It's a delightful and edible gift that's sure to impress.

Funfetti-Inspired Packaging and Presentation

Rainbow Sprinkle Wrapping Paper:

Wrap your Funfetti cake or gift box in colorful rainbow sprinkle-patterned wrapping paper. You can create your own by adhering rainbow sprinkles to plain wrapping paper using double-sided tape or a glue stick. Finish with a ribbon and a small card for a festive and eye-catching presentation.

Personalized Funfetti Cake Topper:

Design and create a personalized cake topper that reflects the occasion or the recipient's name or initials. Use glitter cardstock, wooden cutouts, or even edible materials like fondant or gum paste. Attach the topper to the cake or gift box for a personalized touch that makes the gift extra special.

DIY Funfetti Cake Mix Jars and Gift Baskets

Funfetti Cake Mix Jars:

Fill clean and sterilized mason jars with layers of pre-measured Funfetti cake mix ingredients, including flour, sugar, baking powder, and rainbow sprinkles. Attach a decorative tag with baking instructions and a personalized message. You can also include additional items like mini sprinkle containers or small baking utensils as a bonus. Arrange the jars in a gift box or basket for a delightful DIY Funfetti cake mix gift.

Funfetti Gift Basket:

Create a gift basket filled with Funfetti-themed goodies. Include items such as homemade Funfetti cookies, Funfetti cupcakes, Funfetti sprinkles, and a copy of your favorite Funfetti cake recipe. Add in some colorful kitchen utensils, oven mitts, and a personalized note to complete the gift. The recipient can indulge in Funfetti treats and enjoy the baking experience.

Remember to customize your Funfetti gifts based on the recipient's preferences and the occasion. Whether it's a jar of Funfetti cake mix, a cupcake bouquet, or a gift basket filled with Funfetti delights, these homemade gifts and creative packaging ideas will make your Funfetti cake gift truly memorable and special.

Chapter 20: Funfetti Cake Beyond Baking

In this final chapter, we'll explore Funfetti cake beyond baking. From Funfetti-inspired crafts and DIY projects to Funfetti-themed parties and celebrations, as well as unconventional uses for Funfetti sprinkles, let's embrace the colorful and joyful world of Funfetti in various creative endeavors.

Funfetti-Inspired Crafts and DIY Projects

Funfetti Confetti Popper:

Create your own Funfetti-inspired confetti poppers using empty toilet paper rolls or small cardboard tubes. Fill them with a mixture of rainbow sprinkles and colorful tissue paper confetti. Decorate the outside with colorful paper or washi tape. When it's time to celebrate, simply pull the popper apart to release a shower of Funfetti confetti.

Funfetti Candle Holder:

Transform a plain glass candle holder into a festive Funfetti centerpiece. Apply a layer of craft glue to the outside of the candle holder and sprinkle rainbow sprinkles all over it. Let it dry completely before placing a tea light or small candle inside. When lit, the candle will cast a beautiful and whimsical glow through the sprinkles.

Funfetti-Themed Parties and Celebrations

Funfetti Party Decorations:

Create a Funfetti wonderland for your next party or celebration. Decorate the space with colorful balloons, streamers, and banners. Use tablecloths and napkins in Funfetti-inspired colors. Incorporate

Funfetti-themed table centerpieces, such as glass jars filled with rainbow sprinkles and colorful flowers. The vibrant and joyful atmosphere will set the perfect tone for the celebration.

Funfetti Photo Booth:

Set up a Funfetti-themed photo booth area at your party. Create a backdrop using a large sheet of colorful wrapping paper or a fabric with a Funfetti pattern. Provide props like colorful hats, sunglasses, and sprinkle-covered photo frames for guests to use in their pictures. It's a fun and interactive way to capture memories with a sprinkle-filled twist.

Unconventional Uses for Funfetti Sprinkles

Funfetti Manicure:

Add a touch of Funfetti to your nails by creating a Funfetti-inspired manicure. Apply a clear or light-colored nail polish as the base coat and while it's still wet, sprinkle rainbow sprinkles onto the nails. Gently press the sprinkles into the polish, and once dry, apply a clear top coat to seal the sprinkles in place. It's a playful and eye-catching nail art design.

Funfetti Sensory Bottles:

Create sensory bottles for relaxation or playtime by filling clear plastic bottles with a mixture of colorful Funfetti sprinkles and clear or colored liquids, such as water, oil, or glycerin. Secure the lids tightly and let your little ones shake and explore the mesmerizing movement of the sprinkles inside.

Funfetti cake and sprinkles can bring joy and creativity beyond the realm of baking. Whether you're engaging in Funfetti-inspired crafts, hosting a Funfetti-themed party, or finding unconventional uses for Funfetti sprinkles, embrace the vibrant and playful nature of Funfetti in various creative endeavors. Let your imagination run wild and celebrate the fun and whimsy of Funfetti in new and exciting ways.

In conclusion, the "Funfetti Cake Cookbook 101" takes you on a delightful journey into the world of Funfetti cakes. From understanding the history and popularity of Funfetti to mastering the art of Funfetti cake baking, decorating, and gifting, this cookbook offers a comprehensive guide to creating joyful and delicious Funfetti creations.

With 20 chapters filled with recipes, tips, and ideas, you'll be equipped with the knowledge and inspiration to embark on your Funfetti baking adventures. Explore classic Funfetti cakes, cupcakes, and mini treats, as well as decadent layer cakes and cheesecakes. Discover gluten-free, vegan, and healthier alternatives for those with dietary preferences or restrictions. Get creative with international flavors, boozy treats, and Funfetti-inspired breakfast options.

The cookbook also goes beyond baking, exploring Funfetti in various aspects of life. From Funfetti-themed parties and celebrations to crafts, DIY projects, and unconventional uses for Funfetti sprinkles, you'll find endless ways to infuse the joy and color of Funfetti into your world.

Whether you're a seasoned baker or just starting your baking journey, the "Funfetti Cake Cookbook 101" provides a range of recipes and ideas for everyone to enjoy. So, grab your apron, gather your sprinkles, and let the fun begin! Get ready to create delightful Funfetti cakes that will bring smiles and happiness to every occasion.